# SCHIRMER'S LIBRARY
# OF MUSICAL CLASSICS

# FRIEDRICH SEITZ

# Pupil's Concertos

## For Violin and Piano

ISBN 978-0-7935-3912-3

# G. SCHIRMER, Inc.

DISTRIBUTED BY

HAL•LEONARD®
CORPORATION
7777 W. BLUEMOUND RD. P.O. BOX 13819 MILWAUKEE, WI 53213

Printed in the U.S.A. by G. Schirmer, Inc.

# Pupil's Concerto Nº 2
## First Position

Friedrich Seitz. Op. 13

Printed in the U.S.A. by G. Schirmer, Inc.

Tempo I

Violin

# SCHIRMER'S LIBRARY
## OF MUSICAL CLASSICS

# FRIEDRICH SEITZ

# Pupil's Concertos

## For Violin and Piano

ISBN 978-0-7935-3912-3

# G. SCHIRMER, Inc.

DISTRIBUTED BY

HAL•LEONARD®
CORPORATION
7777 W. BLUEMOUND RD. P.O. BOX 13819 MILWAUKEE, WI 53213

Printed in the U.S.A. by G. Schirmer, Inc.

# Pupil's Concerto Nº 2
## First Position

### Violin

Friedrich Seitz. Op. 13

Printed in the U.S.A. by G. Schirmer, Inc.

# Violin

Adagio

9

Allegretto moderato

8 ad lib.